ADVANCED ENGLISH

HOMEWORK

OLGA CLARKE

Extra Practices
for Private Study

To the Student

This book contains practical exercises on some of the most important points of English. There are several exercises on each point. If you use the book at home on your own it is best if you do one exercise on a particular point at one time, then come back to the others later. In class, do the exercises aloud first, then write them at home. Some of the exercises at the end are just for fun, but are still useful. The answers are given.

Good luck!

© 1981 Language Teaching Publications
35 Church Road, Hove BN3 2BE, England

Reprinted 1982, 1983, 1984
ISBN 0 906717 07 8

Printed in England by Gadds Printers Ltd., Worthing

Contents

Acknowledgements

We are grateful to the following for help in producing this book:
Punch for several cartoons
Nils Lundin and Ake Lindgren for help with some practices
Eva Henricson and Janet Andersson for assistance in typing the manuscript.

There is and It is

Put the appropriate part of *there (be), it/they (be)* **in the spaces in the following:**

A: Jack! _____ someone on the phone for you.

B: Oh, who _____ ?

A: I don't know but I think _____ Dave.

B: **(takes phone)** Hello, is that you Dave?

C: It is. Look, sorry to ring so late but I'm afraid _____ no chance of me picking you up in the morning. _____ something wrong with the car again.

A: Oh dear. What's wrong? _____ the clutch again?

C: No, not this time. I think _____ something to do with the ignition. Anyway, _____ no way _____ be fixed by tomorrow morning so it looks as if I'll have to miss the meeting.

A: _____ any special reason you wanted to be there this time?

C: Well _____ actually, _____ something I wanted to raise. _____ the date of the December meeting. I thought _____ too near Christmas.

A: Well look, _____ no need for you to be there. _____ not a terribly serious matter. Can't I raise it on your behalf?

C: Why not, if you don't mind? But I think _____ impossible for me to get there. _____ more than 20 miles you know, and _____ no buses before 8 o'clock anyway.

A: Look, _____ no problem. _____ easy enough for me to say something. I don't think _____ many people there anyway.

C: No, neither do I, but if _____ any difficulty you can ask Sam to give me a ring. Sorry about the inconvenience.

A: Don't worry, these things happen!

The Article

Some of the following sentences require an article (*a/an or the*) in the spaces. Some are correct without the article. Complete the sentences, adding the article where you think necessary.

1. Concorde can travel at twice _____ speed of _____ sound.

2. _____ British politics has moved to _____ left over _____ last few years.

3. He led _____ life of crime from _____ birth to _____ death.

4. Do you remember _____ day you came out of _____ army?

5. We went to see _____ Westminster Abbey. I think _____ Abbey is a marvellous building.

6. Can _____ foreigners get _____ employment in Britain easily?

7. There's _____ time and _____ place for _____ things like that.

8. _____ smoking is bad for _____ health.

9. All _____ customers were disapointed by _____ news.

10. Invite all _____ family _____ more _____ merrier!

11. There are more facilities now for _____ blind and _____ handicapped.

12. I think _____ people wish _____ government would do something about _____ inflation.

13. _____ cheapest place to get them is a shop on _____ corner of _____ King Street and _____ Hanover Street.

14. They gave _____ dinner for _____ whole staff just before _____ Christmas.

15. Although _____ price has gone up, _____ quality is _____ same as before.

16. I've got _____ tape recorder, but not _____ record player.

17. _____ ignorance of _____ law is no excuse.

18. I got _____ cold in _____ winter. It really was _____ worst I've ever had.

19. There will be _____ reduction of 10% on _____ list price if you can pay by _____ end of _____ month.

20. _____ vandalism is _____ problem for _____ society throughout _____ Europe.

21. Some of _____ England's most spectacular scenery is in _____ Lake District, particularly near _____ Lake Windermere.

22. At _____ school I was quite good at _____ chemistry but not at _____ languages.

23. _____ progress _____ science has made in recent years has astonished even _____ scientists themselves.

24. If there is _____ doubt in your mind about _____ evidence, you must not convict.

The Future

Very often when we speak we don't just 'give the facts of the matter' but the speaker expresses his opinion or attitude to the facts as well.

Look at the following sentences and then at the 'interpretations' underneath.

From each sentence pick the interpretation which you think fits it best.

1. He's going to come.
2. He's coming.
3. He's definitely not coming.
4. He'll never come.
5. He's sure to come.
6. He'll probably come.
7. He won't come.
8. He's very unlikely to come.
9. I'll be surprised if he comes.
10. I'd be suprised if he came.
11. Surely he's going to come.
12. He might come.
13. Perhaps he'll come.
14. He must be going to come.
15. I don't think he'll come.
16. I doubt if he'll come.

Interpretations

If you regard the event as 'he comes' what extra information or attitude does the speaker show in each case. He thinks:

(a) The event is certain to happen.

(b) The event is certain not to happen.

(c) It would be very surprising if the event happened.

(d) It would be very surprising if the event did not happen.

(e) It would be a bit surprising if the event happened.

(f) It would be a bit surprising if the event did not happen.

(g) He doesn't really know what to think.

(h) He knows the event will happen because he's been told (by the person concerned).

(i) He doesn't *know* but he guesses the event will take place.

(j) It would be a good idea if the event took place.

(k) There's no way of knowing whether the event will take place or not.

As you can see, you cannot just pair up the sentences and the interpretations. Sometimes the difference of meaning between two or more of the sentences is so slight that, without more context, it's not possible to give more accurate interpretations.

Must and Have to

Fill in *must, mustn't, have to, don't have to* **or** *don't need to* **in the following. If you think more than one is possible, try to choose the one you think is most natural in the context.**

1. You _____ touch this. It's terribly fragile.

2. You _____ forget to post those letters.

3. We really _____ hurry, it's only 20 past.

4. You _____ take yours, I've got mine.

5. You _____ ask her, she's sure to volunteer anyway.

6. Don't worry, it's no trouble, I _____ to do anything special.

7. You _____ tell the bank, they don't do it automatically.

8. You _____ be surprised if he's forgotten.

9. We _____ take the car - there are no buses after 11 that night.

10. You _____ ask him about his eyes. I'm afraid it still upsets him.

11. You _____ close the gates completely otherwise the lift won't start.

12. You _____ try to carry that - it's far too heavy.

13. You _____ wait for me. I know the way.

14. You _____ give my regards to Gemma and the children.

15. You know you _____ park on double yellow lines, don't you.

16. You _____ worry if he doesn't come today - he's terribly forgetful.

17. You _____ ring back - you'll see me tomorrow anyway.

18. I'm easy, you _____ ask **me.**

19. I _____ remind Jill about the trains this evening.

20. I'll lend you it with pleasure but you _____ let me have it back on Friday.

21. You _____ let me have it back this week, I won't need it.

22. You _____ ask the English what they earn - it seems rude to them.

23. It's a very popular restaurant, so you _____ book a table.

24. You _____ say 'mustn't' when you mean 'don't have to'!

6

Should and Would

Insert *should/would/ought to* **or** *shouldn't/wouldn't* **in the following sentences. Usually there is only one possibility in natural spoken English. Occasionally more than one is possible. If this is so, the various possibilities are given in the Key**

1. I'm surprised to see you! _____ you be at work today?
2. I _____ do that, if I were you.
3. I don't think you _____ tell him yet.
4. I'd be very grateful, if you _____ mind.
5. If you hurry you _____ catch the ten past
6. _____ you like a cup of tea or something?
7. I don't want to, but I think we _____ ask Jane and Peter.
8. If you feel you _____ ring her, you'd better do it straightaway.
9. I _____ be grateful, if you could.
10. I knew we _____ have waited so long
11. It'll be about three miles, I _____ think.
12. If there was any doubt in my mind, I _____ tell you, _____ I?
13. What _____ you do, if you were me?
14. It's quarter to already so the bus _____ be here anytime.
15. I _____ worry, it'll turn up, I'm sure.
16. Who _____ have thought a thing like that could happen?
17. The Government really _____ do something about it.
18. I don't think it _____ help if you told him.
19. I _____ think he knows anything about it
20. In those circumstances people _____ try to help each other.
21. What date _____ it be in by?
22. It _____ be cheaper if we get returns.

"Excuse me but I think you ought to know—you're being eaten."

7

Conditionals

PRACTICE 1

Which of the following combinations are possible?

1. If I'd known,

   a) there would have been no problem
   b) there would be no problem now
   c) I decided earlier
   d) there wouldn't have been a problem
   e) I had told the police
   f) I'd tell the police

2. If you'd disagreed

   a) there was no point in continuing
   b) it was most unfortunate
   c) I had been furious
   d) I would have lost my temper
   e) I was going to leave
   f) I would have left

3. Unless you back down immediately

   a) I'll be resigning
   b) I'm going to resign
   c) I resign
   d) I'm resigning
   e) I'll resign
   f) I'll have to resign

4. If there was a nuclear accident,

   a) a disaster area would be created
   b) you can expect a lot of casualties
   c) I dread to think of the consequences
   d) I had rather not be around
   e) I would rather not be around
   f) there was going to be an enquiry

5. If we hadn't reported it

   a) someone could have been injured
   b) a child could be killed
   c) there might have been an explosion
   d) the police had not known about it
   e) we were not sleeping afterwards
   f) we could not have forgiven ourselves

Often text books teach 3 common combinations (called the first, second and third conditionals) but be careful - this practice will show you that a lot of other combinations are possible too.

PRACTICE 2

Fill in the form of the verb in the following. Only the basic verb is given. In many cases you will have to add the appropriate auxiliaries too.

Sometimes there is more than one possibility. In the key we discuss the different possibilities for natural spoken English.

1. If I were you, I _____ (not stop) seeing her.
2. His wife says that if he _____ (start) smoking again, she _____ (leave) him.
3. What _____ you do if someone _____ (come) up to you and _____ (say) he was your long lost brother?
4. I _____ (not be) prepared to concede unless there was more evidence.
5. If Kennedy _____ (not be) shot, American politics _____ (not be) in the state it is.
6. If this tax _____ (not be) introduced in the sixties, the politicians _____ (contemplate) it today.
7. Unless something _____ (do) pretty soon, there _____ (not be) any future for anyone.
8. If we _____ (not have) the van ten years ago, I don't know what we _____ (do).
9. I'm sure she'd run you, if she _____, but it doesn't look as if she _____ (be) able to.
10. Would there have been the same trouble if I _____ (go) myself?
11. Just imagine what _____ happened, if there _____ (be) a leak.
12. If you _____ (expect) me to fork out for you again tonight, then you _____ (make) a big mistake.
13. Providing he _____ (not drink) anything, he _____ (have) nothing to worry about.
14. Have you ever thought what would happen if you _____ (not lock) the door.
15. You'll find it pretty difficult unless you _____ (do) it before.
16. People _____ be much happier if they _____ (stop) worrying so much.
17. Do you think it _____ been all right if I _____ not been there?
    If I _____ (know) she was going to be there, I _____ (not accept) the invitation.
18. Supposing the interest rate _____ (go) down next week, _____ it have any effect?

9

PRACTICE 3

Look at this example:

I fell in love with her — I married her

If I hadn't fallen in love with her I wouldn't have married her

Combine the following in a similar way:

1. I realised the time — I left

_____

2. We booked early — We got seats

_____

3. She missed the train — I had to drive her

_____

4. The fog lifted — We were able to take off

_____

5. There was a witness — He was acquitted

_____

6. We set off early — We got there on time

_____

7. It began — We stayed

_____

8. I told him — He knew

_____

9. I was convinced by them — I agreed

_____

10. I complained — I got better service

_____

11. The Government acted — Prices rose even more sharply

_____

12. The alarm was raised — The damage was enormous

_____

Gerund or Infinitive

Complete the following sentences by adding either the infinitive or the -ing form of the verb. You will sometimes need to add a preposition or particle too (as in the examples a and c).

a) I forgot *to post* the letter.   *(post)*
b) I remember *asking* you to do it.   *(ask)*
c) I'm really serious *about buying* it.   *(buy)*

1. I'm ashamed _____ I forgot.   *(say)*

2. He's not capable _____ responsibility.   *(take)*

3. They are very anxious _____.   *(please)*

4. I'm afraid I don't feel qualified _____.   *(say)*

5. I'm sure I remember _____ her last year.   *(meet)*

6. He omitted _____ me that even though I finished   *(tell)*

   _____ all his post I still wouldn't be allowed   *(type)*

   _____ before 5 o'clock.   *(leave)*

7. I need _____ the car to the garage, the brakes   *(take)*

   need _____.   *(adjust)*

8. I'd like _____ you it, but I do remember   *(lend)*

   _____ you one before.   *(lend)*

9. It's not worth _____ your time on that.   *(waste)*

10. I was just _____ you.   *(try, ring)*

11. Will you remember _____ him that he agreed   *(remind)*

    _____ me tomorrow.   *(see)*

12. Stop _____! I refuse _____ you worry me.   *(complain, let)*

13. He went on _____ that he wasn't used to _____. *(say, travel)*

14. He wouldn't consider _____ us _____ for ourselves. *(allow, pay)*

15. May I advise you _____ immediately.   *(leave)*

16. I really resented him _____ that to me and I   *(say)*

    can't forgive him _____ me like that.   *(treat)*

17. I have succeeded _____ in touch and I asked him   *(get)*

    _____ you.   *(contact)*

18. You'd better _____ him before he forbids them _____. *(tell, go)*

Mixed Tenses

PRACTICE 1

Fill in the forms of the verbs in the following:

It all _____ (happen) a very long time ago now.... or at least it _____ (seem) a very long time. So much _____ (happen) since then. 1972 it was. Late September. I _____ (remember) it _____ (be) then because the leaves _____ (just begin) to fall outside our bedroom window. In fact, it _____ (be) Saturday 29th. We _____ (be) to a party the night before, and I _____ (feel) a little under the weather. Suddenly she _____ (turn) to me and said — totally out of the blue — you _____ (not love) me.... you _____ (not like) me.... in fact I _____ (not believe) you _____ (ever like) me. I _____ (not know) what to say. It was as if someone _____ (just kick) me in the stomach. I _____ (know) then what I _____ (think) for a long time. I _____ (know) that we _____ (not understand) each other and in fact we never _____. When you _____ (live) with someone for a long time, the little unimportant things often _____ (blind) you. They _____ (keep) your attention occupied and away from the things that really _____ (matter). Up until that morning in September there _____ (be) a truce between us. But it wasn't long before one of us _____ (have to) leave. Neither of us really _____ (try) to do anything about it. We _____ (decide) a long time before not to have a family, so there wasn't that to sort out. A month later she _____ (leave), and we _____ (not meet) since. I _____ (meet) her in Boots yesterday. She _____ (look) happier. While we _____ (talk), I _____ (keep) thinking that perhaps if we had been a bit older at the time, we _____ (try) a bit harder.

12

PRACTICE 2

Fill in the forms of the verbs in the following:

The police could not understand how I was able to remember so much and in so much detail. I _____ (explain) that ever since childhood I _____ (train) myself to observe. My father _____ _____ (always insist) on pointing things out to us when we _____ (go) on those long Sunday walks which I _____ (love) so much. He _____ (always explain) something to somebody! That was why I _____ (have) no difficulty in _____ (remember) the events of Wednesday June 6th.

I _____ (remember) the kind of day it was clearly. It _____ (rain) earlier, but by the time I _____ (walk) down the path past the church, the steam _____ (rise) from the ground. Everything _____ (smell) fresh - one of those rare mornings when you _____ (feel) pleased to be alive. That was why the sight of the woman _____ (run) up the path was so distressing. I _____ (never see) anyone with such a look of fear in their eyes. Her long fair hair _____ (fly) wildly behind her as she _____ (rush) past. I _____ (recognise) her anywhere. It was exactly 4 minutes to nine. I always _____ (catch) the 9.07 and I always _____ (leave) home at 6 minutes to 9. It _____ (take) exactly 2 minutes from my home to the church path if you walk briskly which I always _____. Later I _____ (discover) that the police _____ (look) for a woman with long fair hair. I _____ (not hesitate) for a moment. I _____ (get) in touch immediately.

"HA HA HA HA HA HA HA HA HA HEE HEE HEE HEE HEE HA HA..."

"Thirty years ago I would have pitied him—now I have to admit that I quite envy him."

13

Phrasal Verbs

PRACTICE 1 Verbs with 'up'

Fill in the verbs with the following:

1. I must have forgotten to _____ my watch *up*.

2. I've been asked to _____ *up* what has been said at the end of the meeting. I hope I can _____ *up* enough courage to _____ *up* some of the members for what they really are!

3. Would you mind _____ *up* your office. It is _____ *up* with all sorts of rubbish, and I'm not going to _____ *up* with it any more.

4. Come on! _____ *up*. You did it. I saw you.

5. You'll _____ *up* having to share if you don't book early.

6. You'll never guess who _____ *up* yesterday!

7. There's no need to _____ *up* such a fuss!

8. I'll _____ you *up* at the station.

9. I think you must be mistaken - perhaps you've _____ me *up* with someone else.

10. This policeman _____ *up* in his panda car and asked me what I _____ *up* to.

11. I've been off colour but I'm _____ *up* now thanks.

12. Bill and Jean have _____ *up* I'm afraid. I actually thought things were _____ *up* for them, but it seems she got _____ *up* with him.

PRACTICE 2 Verbs with 'out'

Fill in the verbs in the following:

1. The Union don't _____ *out* industrial action, in fact they are threatening to _____ *out* on strike.

2. I was just on the outskirts when I _____ *out* of petrol.

3. I'm sure we can _____ these problems *out*.

4. I'd only been back two days when I _____ *out* in spots.

5. That _____ *out* what I said about foreign food.

6. I've kept silent long enough. It's now time for me to _____ *out*.

7. She'd been off colour all day then in the middle of dinner she _____ *out*.

8. I wish I had never started this, but I'll have to _____ it *out* with him now. I just hope it _____ *out* all right.

9. His writing is awful. It's impossible to _____ it *out*.

10. These shoes really are _____ *out*, but I don't want to _____ *out* £20 for another pair.

PRACTICE 3 Verbs with 'off'

Fill in the verbs in the following:

1. Oh, stop _____ off. Everyone knows you're the greatest!
2. Wake up! How can you _____ off when the plane is about to _____ off?
3. I asked her to dance but she just told me to _____ off.
4. I'm afraid we've had to _____ off the party. John's ill. We're _____ it off till he's better.
5. Haven't you heard that Eve has _____ off the engagement!
6. Imagine if the BBC were there! What a coup to _____ off!
7. Has the pain _____ off any?
8. I thought Mr Johns would have been hurt, but he just _____ it off as if it were a joke.
9. If those people don't turn it down, I'm going up to _____ them off.
10. That milk I bought yesterday has _____ off already.

PRACTICE 4 Verbs with 'down'

Fill in the verbs in the following:

1. This was my great great grandmother's. It's been _____ down from generation to generation.
2. It's best to _____ down if you know you're wrong.
3. This report is very hard to take. Can't you _____ it down a bit?
4. I'm very disappointed, you've _____ me down badly.
5. She's the sort of person who _____ other people down behind their backs.
6. When she got the news she just _____ down and cried.
7. I didn't get the job. They _____ me down.
8. The government have been _____ down by the consequences of high unemployment.

PRACTICE 5 Verbs with 'in'

Fill in the verbs in the following:

1. Do you mind if I _____ in about 5 o'clock?
2. _____ your shirt in - it looks a mess.
3. He never knocks - just comes _____ in.
4. No, I can't guess. I _____ in. Tell me.
5. Do you think I'm a fool? I can't be _____ in so easily.
6. That was nearly an accident - he just _____ in straight in front of me.
7. I can't go so John's _____ in for me.
8. I know I made a mistake. There's no need to _____ it in.

15

Prepositions

Add the missing prepositions or particles (words like *"of"*, *"for"* and so on) to the following. Usually there is only one choice because the adjective can be followed by a particular particle (at least in a particular context. For example *"interested"* is normally followed by *"in"* - *I'm interested in chess*, though it is also of course possible to follow it with *"to"* - *I was interested to hear of your progress*.)

1. I'm not aware _____ any difficulties. (*also* conscious)
2. I'm not accustomed _____ such cold weather.
3. I think I'm entitled _____ a reduction, aren't I?
4. I'm afraid you're not eligible _____ membership until you are 21.
5. I hope you're not superstitious _____ the date - Friday the 13th?
6. Could I speak to whoever is responsible _____ exports please.
7. With a reduction it's equivalent _____ £32.40 each. (*also* equal)
8. This is not consistent _____ your earlier report.
9. He's very particular _____ time - he hates starting late.
10. This is perfect. It's identical _____ the original one.
11. I'm afraid I'm addicted _____ my pipe.
12. They're very close _____ agreement now.
13. I'm rather doubtful _____ the prospects.
14. That's rather typical _____ his general attitude. (*also* characteristic)
15. I think a lot of people are envious _____ our success.
16. You were wrong _____ the time but right _____ the place.
17. He reminded me _____ Harry Smith. Is he related _____ him?
18. I'm ashamed _____ myself now, but I admit I was suspicious _____ the idea at first.
19. They are well-known _____ their marvellous service. (*also* famous, noted)
20. I'm very grateful _____ you _____ all your help.
21. Who did you say she's got engaged _____?
22. He's very good _____ German and fluent _____ English.
23. They were rather nasty _____ her. (*also* unpleasant, horrible)
24. I'm sorry _____ what has happened. You must be disappointed _____ the results.
25. I agree _____ you. I'm very pleased _____ the results too.
26. I was impressed _____ what he said. It's indicative _____ the right attitude.
27. I think we're all rather uneasy _____ it. (*also* worried, perturbed)
28. We are all very proud _____ you.
29. He is keen _____ tennis, fond _____ golf and interested _____ most sports.
30. He was suspected _____ murder, then accused _____ it. He was acquitted _____ murder but found guilty _____ the burglary.

16

Do and Make

Fill in the appropriate part of (do) or (make) in the following dialogue. Sometimes you will also have to add another word (a 'particle' see page 16) like 'up' 'in' and so on.

A: What do you _____ of Jim?

B: Well, I've really _____ an effort to like him, but I'm afraid I find him a bit odd. He does _____ some very silly things, and yet he has a bad habit of _____ fun of other people's mistakes.

A: You're right. He's _____ a mess of several things recently, but, at the same time he's the sort who'll always _____ you a favour. I can't _____ my mind about him.

B: I know what you mean. Some of his ideas _____ a lot of money for the business but he doesn't _____ a good impression on people. I suppose he _____ his best and he's not as bad as he was, but he doesn't _____ a lot of friends. He's so unreliable.

A: Again, I know what you mean. He _____ a lot of progress in the last few weeks but it is very difficult to tell when he's telling the truth. He _____ so many stories.

B: I know. The other day he _____ that it was his idea to start the sale a few days earlier than we usually do.

A: That _____ me sick. He's always _____ a song and dance about his bright ideas.

B: It _____ him good to hear what people thought about him, you know. It _____ me laugh to think how unrealistic he is about himself.

A: Do you know, it _____ my day if someone turned round and told him the truth!

B: I couldn't agree more. By the way, what have you _____ your hair. It looks different.

A: Yes, well that's a long story!

"What makes you think your husband's engaged a private detective?"

17

'Get'

Get is a very common verb, particularly in spoken English. Fill in the appropriate part of (get) and any particles (words like to, off, into) you need to complete the following examples of natural spoken language.

1. What time do you usually _____ _____?
2. I hope the children didn't _____ _____ _____ any mischief.
3. He's not very good at _____ his ideas _____.
4. He _____ _____ his driving test first time.
5. _____ a move _____! We're in a hurry. _____ _____ _____ it!
6. I tried to ring him, but I couldn't _____ _____.
7. I'm not going to enjoy this, but come on, let's _____ it _____.
8. Nobody knows who did it. Whoever it was is going to _____ _____ _____ it.
9. (On the bus) "Where do I _____ _____ for Harrods please?"
10. You can't _____ _____ _____ the fact that he promised.
11. I tossed and turned last night, I just couldn't _____ _____ sleep.
12. He's trying to _____ _____ Medical School.
13. I keep putting it off but I really ought to _____ _____ _____ some serious studying.
14. This dreary weather really _____ you _____, doesn't it?
15. When did you _____ _____ _____ Majorca?
16. If we're so late, I'd better _____ the car _____ straight away.
17. I don't want to go, but I don't really see how I can _____ _____ _____ it.
18. I know I said I'd do it, but I just haven't _____ _____ _____ it yet.
19. He didn't really understand the situation, just _____ _____ _____ his depth.
20. He's irritating, you know he really _____ my back _____.
21. They're very good friends - they _____ _____ like a house on fire.
22. I've had flu but I'm _____ _____ it now, thank goodness.
23. Is David _____ _____ all right at University?
24. He thinks people are _____ _____ him, but in most cases they are just _____ their own _____ for what he's done.
25. She must be _____ _____ _____ 80, and he's _____ _____ a bit too.
26. I haven't _____ my watch _____ me, but it must be _____ _____ _____ midnight.
27. I've _____ _____ _____ the habit of walking.
28. He keeps looking at her. I think he's trying to _____ _____ _____ her.

18

Reporting

You may have learned to change sentences like this:

>"I'm going to ask my Father"
>
>He said he was going to ask his father.

but, most often in conversation we don't do this. We simply say *"I said ...... and then he said ......"*, **adding the exact words we used. (Sentences like the examples given are, however, normal in** *written* **English).**

There is still a problem in spoken English, though, with sentences like these:

>"Mind your own business"
>
>He told me to mind my own business.
>
>"Don't you think we should ......?"
>
>He suggested we should ......

Here are some more expressions we use in spoken English to *report* **what someone has said.**

He told (me) to/that ......

He ordered (me) to ......

He wondered if ......

He warned (us) that/to ......

He suggested (that) ......

He denied (......ing)

He promised (me) that ......

He reassured (me) that ......

He invited (us) to ......

He recommended that ......

He insisted on/that ......

He threatened to ......

He pleaded (with me) to ......

Now try to report what was said in these examples:

1. Don't wait for me!

_____

2. Be careful!

_____

3. Wouldn't it be best to wait until Saturday?

_____

4. I'm very much afraid that you're mistaken.

_____

5. That's simply not true - definitely not!

_____

6. I most certainly did not say that!

_____

7. If I were you I'd give them another chance.

_____

19

8. Do that, and I'll ring the press.

_____

9. I was very disappointed not to have had a letter.

_____

10. You really should go and see it, I'm sure you'll enjoy it.

_____

11. You may take my word, you'll have it by Saturday.

_____

12. There is no chance, no chance at all, that it is still here.

_____

13. If you're late again, I'll have to report it.

_____

14. You really ought to stop smoking. It's doing you a lot of harm.

_____

15. This is not good enough! I want to see the manager immediately.

_____

16. Come in, come in.

_____

17. Please bring (you, the reader) with you. (S)He'll be very welcome.

_____

18. We are not going to agree. Let's drop the subject.

_____

19. Get out and don't come back!

_____

20. I bloody well will NOT!

_____

21. You'll have to apologise, I'm afraid.

_____

22. Everything will be all right - don't worry.

_____

23. The stuff'll be delivered on time.

_____

24. Please, please wait a while. You're too young yet. Please wait for a while a least.

_____

To get a natural result in some of these examples you will have to do more than just 'report'.

Fill-in Dialogues

Parts of the following dialogues are missing. Complete them.

1. You have just returned to your car. A man is standing beside it. He is angry.

   Him: So you're the one who left this here.

   You: _____ what you're talking about.

   Him: This is private property. You've no right to park here.

   You: _____ I didn't know.

   Him: Hm, that's what they all say.

   You: _____ say I was sorry.

   Him: That's not good enough, I'm afraid.

   You: _____ you're being unreasonable.

   Him: Do you? Well I'm sure I'm not!

   You: Well if _____ I'll be off. Goodbye.

2. Someone has just tapped you on the shoulder. They think they know you.

   Him: Hello, do you remember me?

   You: _____ .

   Him: Oh, of course you do. It was in Miami last year.

   You: _____ I've never been to the States in my life.

   You _____ someone else.

   Him: Oh, I'm terribly sorry. How very _____ me.

   You: Oh _____ .

3. You have just bought something for £4.50. You gave the assistant a £10 note.

   Her: That's 50p back, Sir.

   You: _____ I gave you a ten pound note.

   Her: No it was only five wasn't it?

   You: _____ it was a ten.

   Her: I'm afraid I'll have to call the supervisor.

   . . . .

   Sup: What is it?

   You: Well, this _____ .

   Sup: Are you sure it was a ten pound note?

   You: _____ .

   Sup: You're quite sure?

   You: _____ .

   Sup: Then I must believe you. Could you give the gentleman another £5 please.

   You: _____ _____ a misunderstanding.

4. The following dialogue is more difficult. It's a business situation and there is a lot more to fill in.

A: Good Morning.

B: _____

(meeting with Mr. Duncan arranged for 9.30am)

A: Ah yes. I'm afraid he's been delayed a few minutes.

B: Oh not to worry. I think I'm a few minutes early anyway.

A: _____

(offers a seat; invites B to take his coat off)

B: _____

(keeps his coat on - finds the office rather chilly; asks for a toilet)

A: Certainly, it's just down the corridor, the second door on your right.

B: _____

(returns a few minutes later)

B: _____

(wonders when Mr. Duncan will arrive)

A: Oh, not more than ten minutes, I don't think. Apparently he was caught in the traffic

B: _____

(accepts this information; asks if he may make a phone call - only local)

A: Yes of course. Would you like to use that telephone there.

B: Oh yes, thank you very much.

A: _____

(offers coffee "while B is waiting")

B: _____

(refuses coffee, but says how welcome a cup of tea would be)

A: _____

(doesn't know if tea is available, but will investigate and try to get some)

Mr
D: _____

(apologizes for being late and gives an excuse - the traffic)

B: _____

Is it Appropriate?

If you know a lot of English it is important not only to say what you mean but to try to use the language in the same way native speakers do. Look at the following statements about English and about how it is used. Mark those you think are true 'T', and those you think are false 'X'.

1. *'Morning* is a common more informal variation of *Good Morning.*

2. On somebody's birthday you can say *Happy Birthday* or *Many Happy Greetings.*

3. After you have sneezed the most common thing to say is *Oh sorry.*

4. The most common meaning of *Excuse me* is 'May I have your attention please'.

5. On January 1st or soon after we greet each other by saying _____ *New Year?*

   There are three different words we can put in the space.

6. Someone tells you some bad news. It is natural to say *I AM sorry to hear that* but not natural if you don't stress 'am'.

7. You arrive late for dinner with some friends. All of the following would sound natural: *Sorry I'm late, Excuse me for being late, Excuse my being late.*

8. If you arrive late in England and say, for example, *I'm sorry I'm late* it will seem very odd if you do not also add an explanation of why.

9. Someone apologises to you because they are late (as in 8). The natural answer is *It's all right.*

10. The word 'Please' used completely on its own can mean:
    (a) Yes.
    (b) That's right.
    (c) If you don't mind.

11. A friend has invited you to dinner. In the middle of the meal you can say:
    (a) I like this.
    (b) This is very nice.
    (c) I do like this.

12. You were invited to visit a friend last night. When you meet them today you can say any of the following:
    (a) I enjoyed myself immensely yesterday.
    (b) I did enjoy myself yesterday.
    (c) I enjoyed myself yesterday.

13. Someone has just thanked you for helping them in a small way. *Not at all* is a natural response.

14. The following can mean the same thing:

    (a) By all means.

    (b) Yes certainly.

15. If someone says *I'm afraid I'm not prepared to discuss the matter* it means they are very annoyed.

16. You would use the following in the same situation:

    (a) You know each other, don't you.

    (b) You know each other, do you.

17. *Someone must have closed it, mustn't .....* It is natural spoken English to finish that sentence with either 'he' or 'they'.

18. Some friends have been visiting you for the evening. Now they are going home. It is natural to say *Have a good journey.*

19. Your friends are going on holiday for a few days. It is natural to say *Have a good trip.*

20. It wouldn't be surprising if an English person said each of the following:

    (a) Well, you know, a rose ....

    (b) Ah, a stitch in time, you know.

    (c) Well, a bird in the hand ....

    (d) So, then the cat was in the bag.

21. Customers in a shop often use 'Sir' or 'Madam' to the shopkeeper who will use the same in response.

22. You have been having a conversation on the telephone. The other person says *Anyway* followed by a short pause. It means he is ready to finish the call if you are.

23. English people usually answer the telephone by giving their names.

24. If you order a meal in a restaurant in England you usually order the first two courses (the starter and the main course) at the same time and the dessert later.

25. A friend bought you a coffee the other day. Now you've gone out together for coffee again. He takes out his money, but you want to pay this time. The natural thing to say is *No, no, let me pay.*

26. The following remarks all expect the answer 'No':

    (a) I don't suppose you've got any strawberries, have you.

    (b) You didn't forget to post that letter, did you.

    (c) You won't forget to tell him will you.

    (d) Wouldn't you like something to drink.

27. *You did what!* is a natural way of expressing surprise when someone tells you about something they have done.

28. The following is a normal, natural thing to say in spoken English.

    Yes, I think they must have, mustn't they.

29. You can show disapproval or disbelief in English by saying *Oh he has, has he/Oh they could, could they,* using the appropriate pronoun and auxiliary verb.

30. *I don't care* and *I don't mind* are used in the same way.

31. You can completely change the meaning of *It's quite a big house* depending on whether you put the main stress on *quite* or *big.*

32. You have just met an English person who does not know you, although he knows you are foreign. If he wants to know which town you come from the most natural thing for him to say is *Where are you from?*

33. If you start *Well, to be honest ...,* it usually means you are going to disagree or think the information which follows may upset the other person.

34. The normal English way to spell Cooper is *C-O-O-P-E-R.*

35. You have been talking to a friend and want to send good wishes to a member of his family. You can say, *Give my _____ to (your wife).* There are three different words that can go in the space.

36. You arrive to visit some English friends. When the hostess opens the door, she may say *Welcome* or *You're welcome.*

37. *Sorry?, Pardon?* or *Excuse me?* can all be used to ask someone to repeat what they have just said.

38. It wouldn't be surprising if an English person used each of the following:

    (a) It was a storm in a cup really.

    (b) Ah, well, you know - where angels fear to tread.

    (c) It was a case of too many cooks.

    (d) A miss is as good as a mile.

39. If someone is introduced to you and says *How do you do,* you can reply either *How do you do* or *How are you.*

40. Lots of people, particularly young people, use *Cheers* instead of *Thank you* if you help them in some way.

41. If you stay with an English family overnight, at breakfast someone may ask you *Did you sleep well?* The normal answer is *Yes, thank you, did you?*

42. *I'd rather you didn't* and *No, thank you* are often used with the same meaning.

43. If you meet someone on their 50th birthday you would probably say *Congratulations* to them.

44. You can say the English telephone number 343629 as *thirty-four, thirty-six, twenty-nine.*

45. You have asked for something in a shop. The assistant asks *Did you say ...?* If you answer *Yes* on its own, it sounds very aggressive.

46. Your hostess offers you some more food you can say either *Yes, please* or *Yes, thank you* if you would like some more.

47. If you have visited someone for the evening and want to leave it is normal to say so twice (*I'll have to be going soon, I really must go now* or two similar expressions)

48. *Please* is never used at the beginning of a sentence in spoken English.

49. You answer the phone. The person asks for you, so you say *Speaking.*

50. If someone says *Oh, sorry* after bumping you in a crowded shop it is normal to say *Sorry* yourself too.

51. The opposite of *I'd rather you didn't* is *Yes, of course.*

52. When you put food on the table in front of a guest you say *Here you are.*

53. When you are talking to a friend, you often use *would you* instead of *please* in sentences like *Pass the salt, would you.*

54. The most common phrase to mean 'I want to go back to what we were talking about earlier' is *By the way.*

55. All of the following can mean 'Goodbye' in English: *Cheerio, Bye, So long, I'll be seeing you, Good afternoon, Ta-ta.*

56. You are having a drink with your friends, as you drink you can say any of these: *Cheers, Good health, Bottoms up!*

57. *Please come in* and *Do come in* are both warmer and more friendly than *Come in* on its own.

58. *What's your work* is NOT natural spoken English.

59. When you want a taxi-driver to keep the change, you say to him *That's all right.*

60. When a friend tells you that another friend sends you his regards, you say *send them back, thank you.*

"I'm fairly philosophical about being boiled. What I object to is being dressed."

Responding Positively and Negatively

In the following dialogues you must supply what B says.

1a A: How's your wife?
     B: _____
     A: Good, and the family?

1b A: How's your wife?
     B: _____
     A: Oh really... nothing serious I hope.

2a A: Could I possibly open the window, please.
     B: _____
     A: Thank you very much.

2b A: Could I possibly open the window, please.
     B: _____
     A: Oh well, don't worry, I'll leave it then.

3a A: Is this seat taken?
     B: _____
     A: Thank you.

3b A: Is this seat taken?
     B: _____
     A: Oh, sorry.

4a A: Have you booked, Sir?
     B: _____
     A: And what name was it, please?

4b A: Have you booked, Sir?
     B: _____
     A: Oh, well. Let me see if there is anything free.

5a A: I'm sorry, I think this is my seat.
     B: _____
     A: Oh that's quite all right.

5b A: I'm sorry, I think this is my seat.
     B: _____
     A: Oh you're quite right. I'm most dreadfully sorry.

6a A: I hope you're enjoying your meal, Sir.
     B: _____
     A: Good

6b A: I hope you're enjoying your meal, Sir.
     B: _____
     A: Oh dear. What's the trouble?

7a A: Hello, I haven't seen you for ages, how are you?
     B: _____
     A: Oh very well. What have you been up to lately?

7b A: Hello, I haven't seen you for ages, how are you?
     B: _____
     A: I'm awfully sorry. I thought you were someone I used to work with.

8a A: Could I speak to John please.
     B: _____
     A: Thanks.

8b A: Could I speak to John please.
     B: _____
     A: Oh, never mind I'll ring back.

Agreeing

Look at the following examples:

A: Jack will be there.
B: Yes, so will Andy.
or Will he really? Andy won't.

A: Jack won't be there.
B: No, neither will Andy.
or Won't he? Andy will (be).

A: Andy couldn't make it.
B: No, neither could Jo.
or Couldn't he? I think Jo was there.

A: Sandra'd been very annoyed.
B: Yes, so would Maureen.
or Would she! Maureen wouldn't (have been).

Notice how the second speaker "links" what he has to say to the first speaker's statement. This often involves manipulating the auxiliary verb. It's very easy to do this (slowly!) in a written exercise, but can you do it in spontaneous conversation? And, more important still, do you *do* it? **Practise with these examples until the whole "answer" seems natural and spontaneous to you. (Sometimes the response is more difficult than *just* a manipulation - try to say something *natural*)**

1. Jill and David are definitely not going. (Mary and Steve are not going)

_____

2. The children are free next week. (ours, last week)

_____

3. I won't be taking the car. (I'm not taking mine)

_____

4. I think they must have got caught in the traffic. (Jack too)

_____

5. I can't make head nor tail of this. (It seems straightforward to me)

_____

6. You shouldn't have asked Bill. (who?)

_____

7. It didn't take us long. (Me 2 hours)

_____

8. I wish I'd taken the car. (I didn't take my car, and I'm glad I didn't)

_____

9. I ought to have got a return. (Me too)

_____

10. We'd love to go there. (Us too)

_____

Interpreting Natural Language

Look at the remarks B makes in the following dialogues. Try to interpret what he *really* means - is he angry, sarcastic, facetious or what? You need to consider the information about the speakers *and* what they say. Write down what you think and then check with the key.

A and B are business colleagues. A letter has just arrived from a third person, David Brown.

A: There was a letter from David Brown this morning.

B: (1)   About time too!

A: He's been away and apologises for the delay.

B: (2)   I should think he does. How long is it since we wrote to them?

A: About six weeks.

B: (3)   Exactly.

A: Well we've got a reply now anyway.

B: (4)   And what does the dynamic Mr Brown have to say for himself?

The same people (A and B) are working in the office.

A: Do you think we ought to finish this before lunch?

B: (5)   If you like.

A: I'd rather get it finished - it is rather urgent, you know.

B: (6)   I suppose so.

A: Do you *mind* waiting a bit for lunch?

B: (7)   Not really, no.

A: Come on! It can wait - providing it catches the post today.

B: (8)   But I thought you said you wanted to finish it before lunch.

A: Not if you're going to get uptight about it.

B: (9)   Me!

A: Yes, you.

B: (10) *I* didn't come in at ten o'clock this morning.

A: Very true but we've got better things to do with our time than argue about this.

B: (11) Maybe.

A: You don't sound very convinced.

B: Well I do think it was a bit inconsiderate.

A: Maybe you're right. I'm sorry, really. But can we finish it now so we've got the afternoon clear.

B: (12) Yes OK, providing you buy the drinks with lunch.

A: Its a deal.

Cloze Texts

PRACTICE 1

Fill in one word in each of the blanks in the following texts. Sometimes more than one answer is possible. Make a list of all the possibilities and compare them with the key.

_____ was in the spring of 1894 _____ all London was interested

_____ the murder of the Honourable Ronald Adair in most unusual

_____. The public has _____ learned those particulars of the crime

which came _____ in the police investigation but a good _____ was

supressed on that _____. The case _____ the prosecution was

_____ strong that it was not necessary to bring forward all the facts.

_____ now, after nearly ten years, am I allowed to _____ those

missing _____ which make up the whole of that remarkable chain. The crime

was _____ interest in _____, but that interest was nothing

_____ to the sequel, which gave me the greatest shock _____ any

event in my adventurous life. _____ now, after this long interval, I am thrilled

_____ I think _____ it, and I feel _____ more the same sudden

flood of joy and incredulity which I remember _____ well _____ that

time. _____ me say I _____ have shared my knowledge earlier

_____ _____ prohibited from _____ _____ by Sherlock

Holmes _____.

You can _____ imagine that my friendship _____ Holmes had

interested me deeply _____ crime. After _____ disappearance I

_____ failed to read carefully the reports _____ crime which appeared

in the press. From _____ to _____ I _____ attempted to use his

methods myself, _____ _____ success. _____ was nothing,

_____, which _____ my imagination as much as the Adair murder.

_____ I read the reports I realised more clearly than _____

_____ serious Holmes' death had been _____ the community.

_____ day, as I turned the case _____ _____ my mind,

_____ as I tried I could find no adequate explanation. Let me remind you

_____ the facts.

PRACTICE 2

A: You know Steven Arlen don't you. What do you _____ of him?

B: Not much. I _____ to think how he's got to his present position.

A: I know. The mind _____ but he's as thick as _____ with Ray Reece. And of course he **has** had some good ideas.

B: I'm afraid you're _____ under a _____ there. Most of his ideas have been borrowed from other people. I saw _____ him a long time ago; caught him going through my papers, perhaps not quite _____-_____; he closed the file in the _____ _____ time, but I saw _____ to know what was _____ _____.

A: Well I'm _____ to believe that about anybody but it's a _____ point where the new advert came from. I'd been playing around with an idea rather like it for a _____.

A: The worst is he seems so friendly, you know, direct, calls _____ _____ _____ _____.

B: He certainly doesn't _____ his words, but I couldn't care _____ _____ about that, but it _____ that he got the credit for my idea.

A: He'd probably have got that anyway. He's Reece's nephew isn't he and after _____, _____ is thicker _____ _____.

B: Perhaps he's not as bad as he seems, perhaps a bit of a _____ for the rest of the family.

A: I'm afraid I still think the day he goes will be a _____-_____ day!

B: I'm very much afraid that would be the _____ opinion. I really can't think of _____ who likes him.

"I wish you'd stick to table-cloths."

31

Stress in Long Words

Can you underline the syllable of each of these words which carries the heaviest stress. The stress in long words frequently falls on the syllable third from the end (enJOYable, proHIBitive) but be careful, this is by no means always true!

1. cigarette
2. telephone
3. shampoo
4. apology
5. industrial
6. university
7. necessity
8. inconvenient
9. unnecessary
10. misunderstand
11. vegetable
12. elastic
13. architect
14. carelessness
15. advertisement
16. pedestrian
17. photograph
18. photography
19. photographic
20. temporary
21. mechanical
22. eligible
23. illegible
24. enthusiastic

25. account
26. accountant
27. analysis
28. appreciation
29. coincidence
30. congratulations
31. contribute
32. contribution
33. diplomatic
34. directory
35. economical
36. educational
37. elegant
38. elucidate
39. engineer
40. engineering
41. European
42. expansion
43. fantastic
44. hypochondriac
45. hypocritical
46. important
47. impotent
48. impractical

49. indifferent
50. inhabitant
51. insincere
52. irresponsible
53. laboratory
54. margarine
55. mediocre
56. mountaineer
57. pedantic
58. political
59. politician
60. populated
61. proposal
62. proposition
63. recipe
64. receptionist
65. requisite
66. respectable
67. spontaneous
68. statistical
69. statistics
70. thermometer
71. unanimous
72. unconventional

Note: We have tried to use only words which you may find useful in speaking English. If there are any which you do not know, perhaps you could look them up in your dictionary and find out how to use them.

Just for Fun 1

Elimination Puzzle

In these puzzles you are given clues. Each clue helps you to find two words from the given list which are linked. After finding (and "eliminating") all the pairs, one "odd" word remains.

The clues are of different kinds but two common types are these:

The clue gives a two-word expression which is "the answer" e.g.

ordinary = commonplace, common place

The clue gives a word which occurs in common expressions with two of the words in the list e.g.

Two linked with box   Christmas *box*   pillar *box*

Be careful as sometimes one word in the list may fit more than one clue and if you use it in the *wrong* pair you will find it impossible to find *all* the pairs later in the puzzle!

Clues

a. The place for a travelling snack?

b. People like this always have trouble

c. A circular route?

d. Two kinds of case

e. A biscuit

f. Two words linked with left

g. You won't do anything silly if you use it

h. It means honest and reliable

i. Two crossings

j. Two vegetables

k. The express way to travel?

l. You may have to pay it before you can eat

m. Two linked with stop

n. Two synonyms

o. Two tones your receiver may produce

p. Two cabinets

Words

1. up	12. plane	23. filing
2. car	13. watch	24. charge
3. bus	14. brief	25. buffet
4. book	15. zebra	26. common
5. flat	16. bread	27. handed
6. line	17. right	28. dialing
7. main	18. swede	29. library
8. road	19. short	30. cocktail
9. ring	20. sense	31. engaged
10. cover	21. prone	32. luggage
11. level	22. sprout	33. accident

Just for Fun 2

How many of the following abbreviations do you know? Do you know what they mean (in English, even if some are based on, for example, Latin) and how and where they can be used

1. a.m.
2. p.m.
3. VAT
4. TUC
5. CBI
6. RAC
7. AA
8. IRA
9. CSE
10. GCE
11. EEC
12. YHA
13. RNLI
14. POW
15. PAYE
16. CID
17. do.
18. IOU

And **where** would you find these?

19. PTO
20. RSVP
21. c/o
22. pp
23. LCP
24. RIP
25. PS
26. C/F
27. HB
28. KLM
29. ff
30. Ph.D

Just for Fun 3

Elimination Puzzle

Clues

a. never been used
b. two of the pack
c. two mills
d. you'll have one if you are short of money!
e. ring this for food?
f. two linked with head
g. two sets?
h. two linked with book
i. the holiday shop?
j. two linked with horse
k. two linked with board
l. a fighting holiday?
m. a flower
n. two linked with present
o. two linked with course
p. two linked with sea

Words

1. jet
2. day
3. ace
4. cup
5. new
6. golf
7. ache
8. room
9. jack
10. head
11. gift
12. sick
13. play
14. wind
15. side
16. line
17. main
18. over
19. shelf
20. draft
21. brand
22. credit
23. horse
24. pepper
25. boxing
26. cheque
27. travel
28. butter
29. wedding
30. agents
31. service
32. sandwich
33. birthday

34

Just for Fun 4

Do you know what abbreviation is used in addresses in England for each of the following:

1. Street
2. Road
3. Avenue
4. Gardens
5. Crescent
6. Square

What are the full names of these countries:

1. Worcs.
2. Hants.
3. Notts.
4. Northants.
5. Lancs.
6. Leics.
7. Bucks.
8. Glos.
9. Glam.
10. Herts.
11. Staffs.
12. IoW

Just for Fun 5

Write out fully how you say each of the following if you had to read them aloud:

1. $6 \times 3 = 18$
2. $-3°C$
3. 10.3%
4. $\frac{4}{5}$
5. £24.60 p.a.
6. $V = \pi r^2 h$

Just for Fun 6

Link up the medicine with 'what's wrong':

1. aspirin
2. throat pastilles
3. kwells
4. elastoplast
5. calamine lotion
6. alkaseltzers
7. vick inhaler
8. optrex
9. TCP

a. you've cut your finger
b. you have a bad headache
c. you have a bad throat
d. you have a cold and your nose is blocked
e. you've cut your leg and want to clean it
f. you have a bad tummy
g. your eyes are hurting
h. you have been bitten by insects
i. you need something before you travel on a long journey

Let's hope you never need to ask for these things — but now you know what the things you may need are called — at least in England.

Just for Fun 7

English Proverbs
Every language has its own proverbs. Can you complete the following:

1. A stitch in time saves _____.
2. Too many _____ spoil the broth.
3. A rolling stone gathers no _____.
4. It's an _____ wind that blows nobody any good.
5. A nod's as good as a wink to a blind _____.
6. Make _____ while the sun shines.
7. Don't put all your _____ in one basket.
8. There's no _____ without fire.
9. A _____ in the hand is worth two in the bush.
10. Every _____ has a silver lining.
11. Don't count your _____ before they hatch.
12. Spare the rod, spoil the _____.

Just for Fun 8

This puzzle is slightly different. Of course you know a lot of adjectives to describe people but many common ones are made of two words, sometimes written as a single word, sometimes as two and sometimes with a hyphen. Fill in an adjective like that using two words from the lists each time.

1. He never beats about the bush, on the contrary he's very _____.
2. He didn't take much interest. He seemed very _____.
3. He's not popular because he doesn't speak to anyone else. He's very _____.
4. I'm afraid he's too _____ to see what will happen later.
5. He knows where he's going. He's very _____ about it.
6. It was a very _____ way of doing things, behind everyone's back.
7. People say terrible things about him but he's too _____ to let it worry him.
8. He's terribly old-fashioned and _____.
9. People get upset because he's so _____ and tactless.
10. He won't give any money to help. He's too _____ for words.
11. Don't trust him - he tells different people different stories - he's completely _____.
12. Don't leave any money lying about, someone round here is a bit _____.
13. He has a good salary and so has she. They must be pretty _____.
14. He's pleasant enough, but doesn't take things too seriously. Perhaps he's a bit too _____.
15. He's not very bright, takes ages to catch on. He's a bit _____.
16. Sorry I can't lend you a penny, I'm _____ myself.
17. When he's made his mind up you can't change him. He can be very _____.
18. They have very traditional views - get terribly shocked if you swear - they really are rather _____.

First half		Second half	
off	high	broke	lipped
short	well	witted	going
single	two	forward	minded
flat	dim	hand	hand
light	tight	sighted	handed
tight	under	minded	headed
pig	thick	heeled	laced
straight	narrow	fingered	skinned
straight	easy	faced	fisted

36

KEY

Page 3. There's someone ... who is it ... it's Dave ... there's no chance ... there's something wrong ... is it the clutch ... I think it's something to do ... Anyway, there's no way it'll be fixed ... Is there any special ... well there is actually. There was something ... It is/was the date ... it was too near Christmas ... there's no need ... It's not a terribly ... it's impossible ... It's more than ... and there are no buses ... Look, there's no problem. It's easy enough ... there'll be many people ... but if there is any difficulty.

Page 4. 1. At twice the speed of sound. 2. British politics ... to the left over the last. 3. A life of crime from birth to death. 4. The day you came out of the army. 5. To see Westminster Abbey ... the Abbey. 6. Can foreigners get employment. 7. There's a time and a place for things. 8. Smoking is bad for the health. 9. All the customers ... by the news. 10. All the family - the more the merrier. 11. The blind and handicapped or the blind and the handicapped. 12. I think people/the people wish the government ... about inflation. 13. The cheapest place ... on the corner of King Street and Hanover Street. 14. They gave dinner/a dinner for the whole staff just before Christmas. 15. Although the price has done up, the quality is the same. 16. I've got a/the tape recorder but not a/the record player. 17. Ignorance of the law. 18. I got a/the cold in winter/the winter ... the worst I've ever had. 19. a reduction of 10% on the list price ... by the end of the month. 20. Vandalism is a problem for society throughout Europe. 21. Some of England's ... in the Lake District ... near Lake Windermere. 22. At school ... at chemistry ... at languages. 23. The progress science ... even scientists. 24. If there is doubt/a doubt ... about the evidence.

Page 5. It is not easy to be definite about some of these. The following answers are suggested. 1. (h) 2. (h) 3. (b) 4. (d) 5. (d) 6. (f) 7. (e) or (c) 8. (c) 9. (e) 10. (c) 11. (f) or (i) or (j) 12. (k) 13. (g) 14. (i) 15. (e) 16. (e) or (c)

Page 6. 1. Mustn't. 2. Mustn't. 3. Don't need to. 4. Don't need to. 5. Don't need to. 6. Don't need to. 7. Have to (or must). 8. Mustn't. 9. 'll have to. 10. Mustn't. 11. Have to. 12. Mustn't. 13. Don't need to. 14. Must. 15. Mustn't. 16. Mustn't. 17. Don't have to. 18. Don't need to. 19. Must. 20. Mustn't. 21. Don't have to. 22. Mustn't. 23. Must (or have to). 24. Mustn't (in most examples where we give 'don't need to' you can also use 'don't have to'. If you are going to an English course you might like to discuss any possible differences between these two expressions).

Page 7. 1. Shouldn't. 2. Wouldn't (possibly 'shouldn't' but stronger). 3. Should (possibly 'ought to' but rather old-fashioned). 4. Wouldn't. 5. Should ('ought to' possible but - which seems a little stronger). 6. Would you. 7. Ought to ('should' possible but with 'I don't want to', 'ought to' is more likely). 8. Ought to ('should' possible as in No. 7). 9. Would ('d more likely). 10. Shouldn't ('ought not to have' is very unusual and 'didn't ought to have' is considered either uneducated or facetious). 11. Would or, more likely, should. 12. I'd tell you wouldn't I? 13. Would. 14. Should ('ought to' possible but less likely). 15. Shouldn't ('wouldn't' possible but less likely). 16. Would. 17. Should or 'ought to' for more serious matters. 18. Would. 19. Shouldn't ('wouldn't' possible but unusual). 20. Ought to ('should' possible but seems rather weak.) 21. Should/ought to/would all possible with slightly different meanings. 22. Should/would/ought to all possible with slightly different meanings.
'Should' usually means it is desirable in the speaker's opinion but 'ought to' is stronger - it usually means the speaker thinks it is moral question.

Page 8. Practice 1. All of the following are possible. 1. a, b, d (and f but this is unusual). 2. a, d, e, f. 3. All are possible. 4. a, b, c, e and f are all possible in spoken English. f would be rare in written English. 5. a, c, f. This practice may surprise you but many forms are possible in good spoken English which are not discussed in older more structurally based text books. The examples given are all possible and can all be explained logically. They are not unusual 'exceptions'.

Page 9. Practice 2. 1. I wouldn't stop. 2. He starts ... she'll leave. 3. What would you do if someone came ... and said. 4. I would not be prepared. 5. Had not been shot ... would not be. 6. Had not been introduced ... would not be contemplating it (possible 'would not contemplate'). 7. Is done ... won't be/will not be. 8. Had not had ... we would have done. 9. If she could ... if she is/'ll be/is going to be able to. 10. If I had gone. 11. Would have happened ... had been. 12. Expect ... you are making or expected ... were making/made (both present and past are possible depending on when the sentence was spoken). 13. Does not drink ... 'll have or did not drink ... 'll/'d have. 14. Hadn't locked. 15. Will ... stop or would ... stopped. 17. It would have been all right if I had ... had known ... would not have accepted. 18. Goes ... will or went ... would (in the last example an immediate possibility is represented by the present tense and a more remote possibility by the past. This is typical of the tense forms used in many conditional sentences).

Page 10. Practice 3. 1. If I hadn't realised the time I wouldn't have left. 2. If we hadn't booked early we wouldn't have got seats. 3. If she hadn't missed the train I wouldn't have had to drive her. 4. If the fog hadn't lifted we wouldn't have been able to take off. 5. If there hadn't been a witness he wouldn't have been acquitted. 6. If we hadn't set off early we wouldn't have got there on time. 7. If it hadn't begun we wouldn't have stayed. 8. If I hadn't told him he wouldn't have known. 9. If I hadn't been/wasn't convinced by them I wouldn't have agreed. 10. If I hadn't complained I wouldn't have got better service. 11. If the government hadn't acted prices would have risen even more sharply/wouldn't have risen so sharply (this sentence doesn't quite follow the pattern, the two answers both make sense and show to slight variations on the original pattern). 12. If the alarm hadn't been raised the damage would have been enormous.

Page 11. 1. To say. 2. Of taking. 3. To please 4. To say. 5. Meeting. 6. To tell ... typing ... to leave. 7. To take ... adjusting. 8. To lend ... lending. 9. Wasting. 10. Trying to ring. 11. To remind ... to see. 12. Complaining ... to let. 13. To say ... travelling. 14. Allowing ... to pay. 15. To leave. 16. Saying ... for treating. 17. In getting ... to contact. 18. Tell ... to go.

Page 12. Practice 1. Happened ... seems ... has happened ... remember ... was ... had just begun ... was ... had been ... was feeling ... turned ... do not love ... do not like ... don't believe ... ever liked (you've ever liked) ... did not know ... had just kicked ... knew ... had been thinking ... knew ... did not understand ... had ... live ... blind ... keep ... matter ... had been ... had to ... tried ... had decided ... left ... have not met ... met ... looked/was looking ... were talking ... kept ... would have tried.

Page 13. Practice 2. Explained ... had trained ... always insisted ... went ... loved/used to love ... was always explaining ... have ... remembering ... remember ... had been raining ... was walking ... was rising ... smelled ... feel ... running ... had never seen ... flew ... rushed ... would recognise ... catch ... leave ... takes ... do ... discovered ... were looking ... did not hesitate ... got.

Page 14. Practice 1. 1. Wind. 2. Sum, summon, show. 3. Clearing, cluttered, put. 4. Own. 5. End. 6. Showed/turned. 7. Kick. 8. Pick. 9. Mixed. 10. Pulled, was. 11. Picking. 12. Broken, looking, fed.
Page 14. Practice 2. 1. Rule, come. 2. Ran. 3. Sort. 4. Broke/came. 5. Bears. 6. Speak. 7. Passed. 8. Have, turns. 9. Make. 10. Worn, pay/shell.

Page 15. Practice 3. 1. Showing. 2. Drop/nod, take. 3. Clear/push (there are a number of other not very polite words that will fit in here too) 4. Call, putting. 5. Called/broken. 6. Pull. 7. Eased. 8. Shrugged. 9. Tell. 10. Gone.
Page 15. Practice 4. 1. Handed. 2. Back. 3. Tone. 4. Let. 5. Runs. 6. Broke. 7. Turned. 8. Brought.
Page 15. Practice 5. 1. Look/drop/call. 2. Tuck. 3. Barging (there are other words possible here too, but this is the most common). 4. Give. 5. Taken. 6. Cut/pulled. 7. Standing. 8. Rub.

Page 16. 1. Of. 2. To. 3. To. 4. For. 5. About. 6. For. 7. To. 8. With. 9. About. 10. To. 11. To. 12. To. 13. About. 14. Of. 15. Of. 16. About, about. 17. Of, to. 18. Of, Of. 19. For. 20. To, for. 21. To. 22. At, in. 23. To. 24. About, by. 25. With, with. 26. By, of. 27. About. 28. Of. 29. On, of, in. 30. Of, of, of, of.

Page 17. Make ... made ... do... making ... made ... do... make ... make ... make ... does ... make ... 's made ... makes up ... made out ... makes ... making ... would do ... makes ... would make ... done to.

Page 18. 1. Get up. 2. Get up to. 3. Getting his ideas across. 4. Got through. 5. Get a move on ... get on with. 6. Get through. 7. Get it over with. 8. Get away with. 9. Get off. 10. Get away from. 11. Get to. 12. Get into. 13. Get down to. 14. Gets you down. 15. Get back from. 16. Get the car out. 17. Get out of. 18. Got round to. 19. Got out of. 20. Get my back up. 21. Get on. 22. Get on. 23. Getting on. 24. Getting at ... getting their own back. 25. Getting on for ... getting on. 26. Got my watch on ... getting on for. 27. Got out of. 28. Get off with.

Page 19. In this exercise there is often more than one answer. We have tried to suggest what we think is most natural. 1. He told me not to wait. 2. He told me to be careful. 3. He suggested we waited until Saturday. 4. He said he thought I was wrong. 5. He insisted that I was wrong. 6. He absolutely/ categorically denied saying it. 7. He thought/suggested I ought to give them another chance. 8. He warned me that if I did it he'll ring the press. 9. He complained that I hadn't written to him. 10. He recommended it very warmly/he said we ought to go and see it. 11. He promised it would be here by Saturday. 12. He was positive/adamant that it wasn't still there. 13. He warned me that if I was late again he'd have to report me. 14. He told me it was doing me harm and I'd have to stop smoking. 15. He was furious and insisted on seeing the manager. 16. He invited me in/asked me to come in. 17. He said you'd be very welcome as well. 18. He suggested we drop the subject. 19. He threw me out. 20. He flatly refused (he was quite unpleasant about it). 21. He told me I'd have to apologise. 22. He tried to reassure me. 23. He promised there'd be no delay. 24. He really pleaded with me to wait a bit.

38

Page 21. 1. I'm afraid I've no idea. Is it, oh I'm sorry, I didn't know. Well I DID say I was sorry. I think you're being unreasonable. Well, if you'll excuse me, I'll be off. 2. I'm sorry I'm afraid I don't. I'm afraid I've never been to the States in my life - you must have me mixed up with someone else. How very silly of me. Oh that's quite all right, I've done the same thing myself. 3. I'm afraid I gave. No, I'm afraid it was a ten. Well, this young lady only gave me 50p in change for this, it cost £4.50 and I gave her a £10 note. Yes I am. Absolutely. Thank you very much; I didn't want to complain, I'm sure it was only a misunderstanding.

Page 22. Good morning, I have an appointment with Mr. Duncan for half past nine. Please sit down, perhaps you'd like to take your coat off. Thank you, no, that's quite all right, it's rather chilly in here at the moment. Sorry, have you a toilet please? Thank you very much. Is Mr. Duncan likely to be long? Oh, I see, do you think I could use the phone please - it's only a local call. Perhaps you'd like a cup of coffee while you're waiting. That's very kind of you but I'm afraid I don't drink coffee, but a cup of tea would be very welcome. Oh, I'll afraid I don't know if I can find any tea, but if you hang on a moment I'll just go and check. Good morning, I'm SO sorry I'm late, I'm afraid I got caught in the traffic, it was absolutely awful. That's quite all right, I know how difficult it can be at this time of the morning.

Page 23. The examples which are NOT discussed here were true. Those which were false are explained. 2. 'Many happy returns'. 3. 'Excuse me'. 5. Only one word is possible - 'happy'. 7. Only the first is natural. 9. 'That's quite all right'. 10. This one is true, but only if you find the right situations. Here are three examples: (a) Did you say two coffees and three teas - please. (b) The same as (a). (c) Can I give you a lift to the station - please. 11. (a) is impossible, (b) and (c) are possible. 12. (c) is impossible. You must have one extra word to show special pleasure (in (a) it is 'immensely', in (b) it is 'did'). 16. The second is only used if the speaker is slightly surprised. 17. The normal use here is 'they'. 18/19. These are true but remember 'trip' usually refers to a holiday but 'journey' only refers to the travelling and is therefore normally only used in situation 18. 20. (a) A rose by any other name would smell as sweet. (b) A stitch in time saves nine. (c) A bird in the hand is worth two in the bush. 21. The proverb is 'Then the cat was out of the bag'. 23. They usually give the number. 25. We normally say 'no no let me ...' but nothing else. The 'me' is stressed. 26. The first three expect 'No' but (d) is a way of offering a drink and can certainly be answered Yes! 30. 'I don't mind' leaves the choice to the other person. 'I don't care' means you are not interested and can easily sound negative. 32. 'Whereabouts are you from' is more natural. We prefer 'whereabouts' to 'where' when we are asking for a detailed rather than general answer. 34. It should be 'double O'. 35. There are both are impossible. 36. Both are impossible. The natural thing is only one word 'regards'. 37. The natural thing is 'please come in' or 'do come in' with a stress on the first word. 37. The last 'please come in' is impossible. 39. The answer to 'how do you do' is always 'how do you do'.

41. 'Yes thank you, very well'. 42. The first is a negative answer when you want to refuse permission, the second is a negative answer when someone offers you something. 43. You would say 'Happy Birthday' or 'Many Happy Returns' the same as for any other birthday except perhaps an 18th or 21st when 'Congratulations' is possible. 44. English numbers are normally given one at a time except 'double three'. 48. Please is normally used at the beginning of invitations - please come in, please don't wait for me, but at the end of requests - a pound of tomatoes please, and in the middle if the person has asked for something. 52. You normally use 'here you are' in English only if the person has asked for something. If you are offering it freely (they have not asked) you normally do not say anything at all. 58. This is true - the most natural expression is 'what do you do for a living'. 60. This sounds very funny. The natural thing to say is 'Oh thank you, that's very kind of him, please give him mine when you see him next time'.

Page 27. 1a. Oh very well thank you. b. Oh I'm afraid she hasn't been too well recently. 2a. Yes of course. b. I'd rather you didn't if you don't mind. I find it a bit chilly in here. 3a. No I don't think so. b. I'm afraid it is. 4a. Yes, yes I have. b. I'm afraid not, no. 5a. Oh I'm so sorry, how silly of me. b. I don't think so, this is (B47). 6a. Yes, very pleasant thank you. b. Well, perhaps a bit disappointing. 7a. Oh fine thanks, and how are you. b. I'm sorry I think you must have made a mistake, I don't think we know each other. 8a. Yes, just a moment, I'll just call him. b. I'm afraid he isn't in at the moment. Can I take a message?

Page 28. 1. Oh aren't they, neither are Mary and Steve. 2. Oh are they, ours were free last week. 3. Oh won't you, neither will I. 4. Yes, so must Jack. 5. Can't you, it seems straight forward to me. 6. Shouldn't I, who should I have asked. 7. didn't it, it took me about two hours. 8. Do you, I didn't. 9. Yes, so should I. 10. Yes, so would we. take mine and I'm glad I didn't.

Page 29. 1. It has been a long time - too long. 2. It would have been unreasonable for him not to apologise. 3. There you are! That is evidence that my opinion was true. 4. Using 'Mr.' here is sarcastic. Adding a positive adjective (dynamic) in a negative context makes it very sarcastic. 5. This depends very much on intonation. It would mean 'I don't mind' or 'I don't really want to but I will if you insist'. It is clear from the rest of this dialogue that (b) means the second of these in this case. 6. I don't really agree. This has a very negative effect combined with No. 5. Both 5 and 6 would be positive if B added another phrase, for example 'If you like, I'm not really hungry, I had rather a lot for breakfast'. 7. In the context of the previous answers this means the exact opposite of what is said. Here it clearly means 'Yes, I do mind waiting'. 8. B is obviously looking for an argument. A keeps trying to compromise but B refuses to compromise. This is a typical way of opening an argument in English. 9. Used alone 'me' nearly always means 'Maybe you're right'. When more words are added to 'maybe' or 'perhaps' it usually means 'I DO agree with you - or at least I think I do'. 10. Stressing 'I' has the same sort of effect - it's not my fault, it's yours. 11. 'Maybe' (or 'perhaps') used alone in English always means 'I do NOT agree and I do not want to discuss it'. It always means the other person is unhappy with the situation and rather annoyed about it. Contrast this answer with A's answer 'Maybe you're right'. 12. This is a typical way of accepting an apology in English - B shows he accepts the apology and shows his friendship towards A by making a further demand on him in a rather light-hearted way.

Page 30. Practice 1. Here is a suggestion for the Cloze test. In some cases you will have found other alternatives.

It was in the spring of 1894 and all London was interested by the murder ... unusual circumstances. The public has already learned ... came out in the police investigation, but a good deal was supressed on that occasion. The case for the prosecution was so strong ... now ... allowed to reveal those missing links ... The crime was of interest in itself, ... nothing compared to the sequel ... shock of any event ... even now...thrilled when I think about/of it, and I feel once more ... I remember so well from that time. Let me say I would have shared my knowledge earlier if not prohibited from doing so by Sherlock Holmes himself.

You can well imagine that my friendship with Holmes ... in crime. After his disappearance I never ... of crime ... From time to time I even attempted... with little success. There was nothing, however, which excited... When/as I read ... than ever how serious ... for the community. Each/every day as I turned the case over in my mind, much as I tried ... of the facts.

Page 31. Practice 2. What do you think/make of him, I shudder to think, the mind boggles, as thick as thieves, you're labouring under a misapprehension, I saw through him, not quite red-handed, in the nick of time, I saw enough to know what was going on, I'm loath to believe, it's a moot point, for a while, calls a spade a spade, he doesn't mince his words, I couldn't care two hoots about that, it rankles, after all blood is thicker than water, a scapegoat, a red-letter day, the general opinion, anyone.

Page 32. 1. cigaRETTE. 2. TElephone. 3. shamPOO. 4. aPOlogy. 5. inDUStrial. 6. uniVERsity. 7. necESSity. 8. inconVENient. 9. unNECessary. 10. misunder- STAND. 11. VEGetable. 12. eLAStic. 13. ARchitect. 14. CARElessness. 15. adVERtisement. 16. peDEStrian. 17. PHOtograph. 18. phoTOgraphy. 19. photoGRAPHic. 20. TEMporary. 21. meCHANical. 22. ELigible. 23. ilLEGible. 24. enthusiAStic. 25. ACCOUNT. 26. aCCOUNtant. 27. aNALysis. 28. appreciation. 29. coINcidence. 30. congratuLAtions. 31. CONtribute or conTRIbute. 32. contriBUtion. 33. diploMAtic. 34. diRECtory. 35. ecoNOMical. 36. eduCAtional. 37. ELegant. 38. eLUcidate. 39. engiNEER. 40. engiNEERing. 41. EuroPEan. 42. exPANsion. 43. fanTAStic. 44. hypoCHONdriac. 45. hypo- CRItical. 46. imPORtant. 47. IMpotent. 48. imPRActical. 49. inDIFFerent. 50. inHABitant. 51. insinCERE. 52. irresPONsible. 53. laBORatory. 54. MARgarine. 55. mediOcre. 56. mountainEER. 57. peDANtic. 58. poLItical. 59. poliTIcian. 60. POPulated. 61. proPOsal. 62. propoSItion. 63. REcipe. 64. reCEPtionist. 65. resPEctable. 66. resPEctable. 67. sponTANeous. 68. staTIstical. 69. staTIStics. 70. therMOMeter. 71. uNANimous. 72. unconVENtional.

Page 33. Just for Fun 1. (a) 25 2, (b) 33 21, (c) 9 8, (d) 4 14, (e) 19 16, (f) 27 32, (g) 26 20, (h) 1 17, (i) 11 15, (j) 18 22, (k) 7 6, (l) 10 24, (m) 3 13, (n) 5 12, (o) 28 31, (p) 23 30. The odd word is 29 library.

Page 34. 1. In the morning. 2. In the afternoon. 3. Value added tax. 4. The Trade Union Congress. 5. The Confederation of British Industry. 6. The Royal Automobile Club (a motoring organisation). 7. The Automobile Association (the other motoring club). 8. The Irish Republican Army. 9. The Certificate of Secondary Education (an examination taken at 16 in England). 10. The General Certificate of Education (a more difficult exam taken at 16). 11. The European Economic Community (The Common Market). 12. The Youth Hostels Association. 13. The Royal National Lifeboat Institution. 14. Prisoner of war. 15. Pay- as-you-earn (the system by which tax is deducted directly from your wage or salary). 16. Criminal Investigation Department (of the police). 17. A short form of 'ditto' meaning 'the same'. 18. I owe you. 19. At the bottom of a page. 20. On a formal invitation. 21. In an address. 22. At the end of a letter. 23. In a cinema advert. 24. In the announcement of a death. 25. After the signature on a letter. 26. At the top of a column of figures. 27. On a pencil. 28. On an aeroplane (it's Dutch airlines). 29. On a piece of music. 30. After someone's name (doctor of philosophy).
Just for Fun 3. (a) 21 5, (b) 3 9, (c) 14 24, (d) 18 20, (e) 8 31, (f) 7 16, (g) 1 10, (h) 19 26, (i) 27 30, (j) 11 13, (k) 15 32, (l) 25 2, (m) 28 4, (n) 29 33, (o) 6 17, (p) 12 23. The odd word is 'credit'.

Page 35. Just for Fun 4. 1. St. 2. Rd. 3. Ave. 4. Gdns. 5. Cresc. 6. Sq. 1. Worcestershire. 2. Hampshire. 3. Nottinghamshire. 4. Northamptonshire. 5. Lancashire. 6. Leicestershire. 7. Buckinghamshire. 8. Gloucestershire. 9. Glamorgan. 10. Herfordshire. 11. Staffordshire. 12. Isle of Wight.
Just for Fun 5. 1. Six times three equals eighteen. 2. Minus three degrees centigrade. 3. Ten point three per cent. 4. Four fifths. 5. Twenty four pounds sixty per annum. 6. V equals pi r squared h.
Just for Fun 6. 1. b. 2. c. 3. i. 4. a. 5. h. 6. f. 7. d. 8. g. 9. e.
Just For Fun 7. 1. Nine. 2. Cooks. 3. Moss. 4. Ill. 5. Horse. 6. Hay. 7. Eggs. 8. Smoke. 9. Bird. 10. Cloud. 11. Chickens. 12. Child.
Just for Fun 8. 1. Straight forward. 2. Off hand. 3. Tight lipped. 4. Short sighted. 5. Single minded. 6. Under hand. 7. Thick skinned. 8. Narrow minded. 9. High handed. 10. Tight fisted. 11. Two faced. 12. Light fingered. 13. Well helled. 14. Easy going. 15. Dim witted. 16. Flat broke. 17. Pig headed. 18. Straight laced.

40